THROUGH KATRINA'S EYES

Poems from an Animal Rescuer's Soul

10-Digit ISBN 1-59113-867-1
13-Digit ISBN 978-1-59113-867-9

Printed in the United States of America.

Booklocker.com, Inc.
2006

THROUGH KATRINA'S EYES

Poems from an Animal Rescuer's Soul

Ed Kostro

Dedication

This Book of Remembrance
Is dedicated to every Katrina victim,
Both human and nonhuman,
Both living and deceased,
Who endured a hellish nightmare
That most of us can only imagine;
And to the many compassionate souls
Who rushed to assist them,
In whatever way they could.

Table of Contents

Preface

I thought I knew what tragedy was until that horrendous day in August 2005 when Hurricane Katrina struck America's Gulf Coast.

As millions of us around the world watched the horror and the heartbreak of this monstrous storm unfolding before our eyes on television, thousands of us felt compelled to offer assistance – in some small way - in any way we could.

And thousands of individuals soon rushed to Louisiana and Mississippi to assist both Katrina's human victims and her many animal victims.

I happened to be one of the thousands who felt compelled to help our nonhuman neighbors – the devoted loving dogs and cats who had been tragically 'left behind' to fend for themselves in this horrendous storm, and in the truly devastating days and weeks and months which followed it.

I met many remarkable people on my journeys south. Some of these individuals belonged to organized rescue groups, some traveled in teams, and some traveled alone – but they were all drawn like a magnet to the ravaged Gulf Coast – as was I.

And most of us never consciously thought about it; we just felt compelled to go. And when many of us informed our spouses that we were, in fact, going, many of our extremely understanding mates simply responded, "I know."

As I think about it now, the actions of thousands of individuals in the wake of Hurricane Katrina remind me of the actions of the subconsciously driven characters in the classic Steven Spielberg movie, '*Close Encounters of the Third Kind*,' in which mankind first makes direct contact with visitors from another world.

The main characters in this movie feel inherently compelled to travel to a certain rock formation in Wyoming; they keep seeing this rock in their dreams; they keep drawing pictures of this rock in their minds, and in their hearts, and in their souls. And they soon travel to Wyoming, where they do encounter these galactic visitors.

In the early days of September 2005, many of us felt inherently compelled to assist the victims of Hurricane Katrina in some way: we kept seeing America's devastated Gulf Coast on television; we kept envisioning the people and the animals there fighting for their lives; we kept picturing these people, and these animals, in our minds, and in our hearts, and in our souls. And we soon traveled to the Gulf Coast.

And for the majority of us, the close encounters we had with both the human victims and the pet victims of this horrendous violent storm, have changed us forever.

I thought I knew what tragedy was, until I looked into the eyes of Katrina's many victims - the eyes of both her human victims, and her animal victims.

The eyes I saw on the Gulf Coast after Hurricane Katrina laid waste to New Orleans and many other coastal cities and towns were haunted, traumatized, helpless, forlorn, and often, completely devoid of hope.

I could only imagine the trauma that both these people and these animals must have endured in that storm, and the trauma, and the heartache, and the terrible numbing fear and sense of total abandonment that far too many of them had to endure for weeks and weeks after this massive storm passed.

I have wept more in the last few months than I have wept in my entire life – and so have many others who traveled to that devastated Gulf Coast in the early days of September 2005 and beyond.

The eyes of the numerous rescuers I saw in the aftermath of Hurricane Katrina were often exhausted, heartbroken, blood-shod, and tear-stained; but yet, filled with utter joy after each and every triumphant rescue.

The eyes of the numerous dogs and cats I encountered were at first completely traumatized; then they would brighten a little after some compassionate care; then very sadly, they would often eventually dim again, as these devoted heartbroken 'left behind' creatures waited and waited for the person they loved with their entire essence to somehow find them, and take them home.

And the eyes that I saw in both Katrina's human victims and in their pets on numerous joyous reunion occasions I was blessed to witness, were the happiest eyes that I have ever seen – on any living beings on this planet.

It was all these sets of eyes, and their vast ranges of emotion, that kept me constantly journeying back to the Gulf Coast – I couldn't stay away.

And there were thousands just like me – who had this same compelling instinctive urge – to return again and again – to help just one more victim, if we possibly could.

They say that our eyes are the windows to our soul, and I now firmly believe that, as do many others who peered into these Katrina eyes.

The following pages depict some of my thoughts and emotions during our pet rescue efforts, and they contain some of the stories of the remarkable souls I encountered on my Katrina journeys, both human and animal.

And as I did when I wrote *Curious Creatures-Wondrous Waifs, My Life with Animals*, I shed a few tears while recalling some of the more tragic tales in this book. And I think you might, too.

These are the stories of the victims and of their rescuers whose eyes I will remember for the rest of my natural days.

Through Katrina's Eyes

"Our eyes,
Are the windows to our soul."

Immanuel Kant

Kant said that our eyes
Are the windows to our soul
After having been to the Gulf
I truly believe that this is so

The images that I now carry
In the back of my troubled mind
Are mostly those of the victims' eyes
Both human and those of the pet kind

As I wandered a large department store there
Searching for much needed pet rescue supplies
I was struck with the look of dazed confusion
In many of the local resident shoppers' eyes

As they slowly shuffled from aisle to aisle
Most of them couldn't decide just what to buy
Which items should be placed into that cart first
They had to start over – they somehow had to try

Should they purchase knives and forks and plates
So that their family members could once again eat
Or should they first get their very sad little boy or girl
At least one tiny new toy or perhaps something sweet

Time seemed to stand still for me as I watched them
I tried very hard to imagine the hell they were now in
The images of those dazed human eyes in that store
Keep vividly coming back to me over and over again

And the terrified eyes of the many dogs and cats I saw
When they were first brought to our pet rescue enclosure
Is something that will be etched into my mind until I die
They run through my mind like a movie – over and over

One minute they were leading normal dog and cat lives
Very content to be with their humans on a very typical day
And within only minutes sheer hell had broken loose for them
Left behind in their homes or swimming for their lives in the fray

But even more firmly etched into the back of my mind's eye
Are the looks of sheer hope as they nervously sit in their pens
Anxiously watching each and every new human approach them
For countless hours each and every day – then over and over again

But when they eventually realize the human approaching them
Is not the one they are waiting for a darkness soon fills their eyes
And that's when my heart and my soul truly begin to ache for them
That's when I begin to lose control - and that's when I begin to cry

The Old Man and His Dog

***"He is my other eyes that can see above the clouds;
My other ears that hear above the winds.
He is the part of me that can reach out into the sea.
He is my dog…"***

Gene Hill

On my first trip down to the Gulf Coast
As I headed east along a rural highway
I came upon two very forlorn figures
Who happened to be traveling my way

So I quickly pulled up along side them
And quickly offered both of them a ride
The old man thought about it for a long while
He looked exhausted but he still had his pride

But eventually he agreed
And he hobbled into his seat
His clothes were ragged and torn
Bloody bandages adorned his feet

His old dog didn't look much better
With matted fur and very weary eyes
As we now drove off the old man spoke
And his very sad tale made me want to cry

"I lost my home in that storm,
Old Max here saved my life;
He's been takin care of me,
Since the day I lost my wife.

"I thought for sure that I was a goner,
I started goin down in that rough sea;
But Maxie here, he had other ideas,
He pulled me out to safety, ya see.

"And now, my legs are all banged up,
And neither of us has eaten in a while;
But me and old Max here are still alive,
Which kinda makes me wanna smile."

I offered him a sandwich and a coke
And I gave old Maxie some dog food
The old man couldn't thank me enough
He said that I had brightened their mood

I soon left them in a small town
Where he said they would be okay
I'll never forget these two survivors
Until my very own dying day

The Woman and Her Daughter

***"We make a living by what we get,
We make a life by what we give."***

Winston Churchill

As I pulled into a gas station
I saw them just sitting out there
It was a woman and her young daughter
At both of them I couldn't help but stare

They were both bundled up in blankets
A few possessions were all they now had
Yet they were smiling and hugging each other
Two homeless folks who seemed awfully glad

As I soon stepped out of my supply-filled truck
The little girl jumped up waved and smiled at me
Then she ran up and asked if I had come to help animals
And when I responded that I had she smiled again with glee

I learned that their apartment had completely flooded out
About all they had left now were a few things and each other
And I also soon learned how this little girl truly loved animals
"But she couldn't have one in our apartment," said her mother

That's when the young girl looked in the back of my truck
And soon spotted my tattered old canvas tent sitting there

"Is that what you're gonna sleep in whiling helping animals?"
And now it was this very needy young girl's turn to stare

So I yanked that old tent of mine out of my truck
And soon set it up for them in a green field nearby
That ecstatic little girl now hugged and kissed me
And huge tears of joy welled in her mother's eyes

As I drove off that very muggy Mississippi day
I realized that it truly is the simple things in life
That can truly make people just a tad happier
Even in their most horrendous times of strife

Katrina's Highway

***"If you pick up a starving dog and make him prosperous,
He will not bite you.
This is the principle difference between a dog and a man."***

Mark Twain

Driving down a Gulf highway
Something on the road ahead
It looked like some sort of dog
But was it really alive or dead

I quickly stopped my old truck
And scooped him up in my arms
This Rottweiler was still breathing
Yet another victim of Katrina's harm

I raced him to the pet rescue camp
And after some fluids he seemed okay
He soon turned into a joyous little pup
And we quickly named him 'Highway'

This docile young dog is now back on his feet
And he loves to romp in the sweet green grass
Thankfully we think that now he'll be just fine
Although it looked like he'd been fading fast

There are thousands of pets like Highway
Sadly wandering all along the Gulf coast
And reuniting them with their former owners
Is something that we rescuers crave the most

But many dogs and cats just like Highway
Will never be reunited with their owners again
And they will soon desperately need foster homes
So all across this vast nation they will have be sent

If you can possibly find it in your heart and soul
To give one of these many storm orphans some refuge
Please contact your local animal welfare organization
Pets also deserve sanctuary from this horrendous deluge

Pet Rescue Camp

"When we honestly ask ourselves which friend in our lives means the most to us,
We often find it is those who, instead of giving advice, solutions, or cures,
Have chosen rather to share our pain,
And who touch our wounds with a warm and tender hand."

Henri Nouwen

I spent many of my hours
Down on the Gulf Coast
At a truly marvelous place
One I now treasure the most

It was located down in rural Mississippi
About ninety miles north of New Orleans
And it contained hundreds of 'left behind' pets
Rescued from streets that were flooded and mean

And it also contained many dedicated people
Drawn like a magnet to these animals' plight
Here I truly witnessed many incredible things
Here I saw people toiling hard both day and night

Here I saw hundreds of forlorn dogs and cats
That were brought in each and every day
And here is where I saw them cared for
In a most loving and compassionate way

De-hydrated dogs and cats that were dying
Sick and injured animals so terribly weak
But each and every dedicated individual here
Made the plight of these pets a little less bleak

I truly made many wonderful friends here
And I witnessed reunions that were grand
When a joyous human found their dog or cat
When a joyous pet found its woman or man

And many of the truly dedicated souls here
Kept returning here time and time again like me
There was just something in these forlorn pets' eyes
That for many of the rescuers here would last an eternity

It's a Bug's Life

"Oh that teenie, weenie thing
They call the lovebug;
Nobody's ever seen it,
But it's got the whole world shook up;
It all started with a little bitty kiss and a hug,
It's the little itty, bitty, teenie, weenie thing,
They call the lovebug."

Lovebug,
George Strait

I had just exited the enormous interstate highway
I was heading down a green tranquil country lane
When suddenly I couldn't see two feet in front of me
My vision was now blocked by a mysterious black rain

I immediately pulled over to the side of the road
Jumped out of my truck and peered into the dark sky
And within only seconds both my hair and my clothes
Were covered with tiny creatures with red bulging eyes

When I eventually pulled into the pet rescue camp
Several people I knew rushed up and gave me a big hug
And as I peered all around this place that I now truly loved
They shouted, "Ain't it great to be here with these love bugs?!"

And now I truly did begin living with thousands of these flies
Who mate feverishly in the south in the spring and in the fall
As they now continued to rain down on all of us for a few weeks
Glued to each others' tiny bodies in their annual Love Bug Ball

And like the many other volunteers who now worked here at camp
I soon adjusted to residing with thousands of these tiny black flies
We all lived and worked and ate and slept and laughed and cried
With these tiny bugs with only love in their tiny love bug eyes

The Maine Man

"Until he extends the circle of compassion
To all living things,
Man will not find peace."

Dr. Albert Schweitzer

I met a very compassionate man from Maine
Whose dauntless mission was extremely plain
He would stay down on the ravaged Gulf Coast
Rescuing these animals that he loved more than most
Through both the scorching heat and the freezing rain

He was up and eagerly ready to go each dawn
While many of us in camp still let out a yawn
And he would spend twenty hours each day
Assisting these left behind pets in every way
Now - three rescued dogs frolic on his lawn

And There Were Hundreds of Volunteers
On the devastated Gulf Coast
Who Were Just Like
This Very Dedicated
Maine Man

Message in a Bottle

"If there is magic on this planet,
It is contained in water."

Loran Eisley

Joe arrived at the pet rescue camp
And he was rip roarin ready to go
Several of us old timers laughed
And yelled, "Joe, ya gotta go slow!"

"The heat down here is brutal,
It's a hundred and ten in the shade;
Drink a bottle of this ice-cold water,
Or how about some of this Gatorade?"

Joe never listened to our sage advice
And he began working extremely fast
Soon the old building housing the felines
With Joe's help was air-conditioned at last

Joe was truly one of the tireless volunteers
And he made a remarkable rescue one day
He lured a terrified Rottweiler out of hiding
With some refreshing ice-cold water in a tray

And the dog Joe rescued also had a tiny bottle
It was wrapped around its neck with a plea,
'Please save my wonderful dog, Himie,
And give him this eye medicine for me.'

Obviously eager volunteer Joe was a whole lot wiser
Than many of us camp old timers on his very first day
He must have saved that very first bottle of water for Himie
So to our very good friend, Joe, we say, "Hip Hip Hooray!"

And if I ever meet tireless old Joe again
I'd like to share another bottle with him
But this time instead of ice-cold water
Perhaps we can sip some whiskey or gin

Miracles in the Mash Unit

"I hope to make people realize how totally helpless animals are,
How dependent on us,
Trusting as a child that we will be kind and take care of their needs...
They are an obligation put on us, a responsibility we have no right to neglect,
Nor to violate by cruelty."

James Herriot

Besides having dedicated rescuers and caretakers and groomers
This pet rescue camp also had extremely devoted techs and vets
Who freely gave their time and medical expertise to these animals
And they are some of the most compassionate individuals I've met

They practiced veterinary medicine in a primitive Mash Unit
Where the severely ill and injured rescued animals were treated
And they very often worked through an entire exhausting night
Until each and every last emergency animal case was completed

On several occasions I had the privilege of assisting them
As they worked to save an extremely traumatized pet's life
And it truly was amazing and uplifting for me to watch them
As they skillfully eased an animal's suffering reducing its strife

And I will never forget one particularly sad evening
When I carried a massive brown chow dog into them
He was covered from head to tail in oil and toxins and tar
And he was so terribly de-hydrated he was about to give in

He had been found huddling under an old motor home
With two of his old canine friends who'd also survived
But the three of them were now barely hanging on to life
And they were surrounded by ten dogs who had already died

As I held this forlorn left behind creature on the treatment table
The tech skillfully began shaving off most of his filthy matted hair
And the compassionate veterinarian soothingly talked to this dog
As she gave him life-saving fluids and needed injections with care

I stopped in at the Mash Unit several days later
To check on this extremely ill and very near death pet
And I simply could not believe my now joy-filled eyes
When I saw him prancing with his friends – and this vet

Mr. Mom

"Dogs are not our whole life,
But they make our lives whole."

Roger Caras

Life at these Katrina pet rescue camps
Was quite different for most and truly unique
We volunteers had given up our modern comforts
To spend time helping creatures who couldn't speak

Some now slept in tents on the cold hard ground
Others tried to sleep in their vehicles every night
Most of us toiled endlessly from dawn until dusk
There was so much to do but for us it seemed right

Dog kennels and holding pens had to be built
The rescued felines needed shelter from the heat
Supplies had to be organized and crates cleaned
And of course hundreds of animals needed to eat

We all gladly volunteered for the necessary tasks
So one day I volunteered to care for forty canines
And by the end of the week that I 'mothered' them
I considered each of them a family member of mine

I truly got to know each of their unique personalities
I brought them all food and water each and every day
And quite often while I was cleaning out their dog runs
Some of my mischievous 'children' would decide to play

And soon I would inevitably be playfully pounced upon
Often I would get knocked over from behind with a thud
And like everyone else who spent time being a 'Mr. Mom'
My clothes would be covered with saliva dog poop and mud

So each and every evening at most of these pet rescue camps
When everyone gathered for dinner following the setting sun
We could all usually tell who had been a 'Mr. Mom' that day
And keeping our distance we would shout, "Bet that was fun!"

And it truly was a fun and rewarding experience for most of us
Even though our clothes often reeked from dirt and doggy poo
But after bonding with these adorable dogs who became our family
We all now miss these children of ours - as most loving mothers do

A Little Flower

"Just living is not enough…
One must have sunshine, freedom,
And a little flower."

Hans Christian Anderson

She had been aimlessly wandering
The flooded streets of New Orleans
She was a tiny frightened tortoise shell
Life for her had been tragically mean

She was emaciated and forlorn
None of her siblings had survived
She stared morosely from her cage
As if she hadn't a single friend alive

But every time that I passed her way
I heard an extremely timid little 'yap'
So every time that I passed her way
I stopped and placed her on my lap

And as I gently stroked her long matted fur
She would very sadly gaze up into my eyes
This tiny brown kitten had touched my soul
This lonely creature had made me want to cry

So on my very last day at the pet rescue camp
I gently picked her up and placed her in my truck
And as we drove off together I named her 'Flower'
Hoping she would blossom with a little TLC and luck

Miss Salsa

"Time Spent With a Cat,
Is Never Wasted.

Colette

This family had lost everything
In the devastation of the hurricane
Now their days were extremely sad
Filled with darkness and with pain

They were now staying with relatives
In a small town in southern Mississippi
At least they'd found their precious Miss Salsa
This old black cat had always filled them with glee

Soon they decided that they would re-locate
To a northern city by the name of Chicago
They were now finally ready to begin their new lives
Until they unbelievably heard that Miss Salsa couldn't go

"We, the Government, will pay the bus fare,
For your family to now re-locate to Chicago;
But, we, the Government, will not pay for a cat,
Therefore, your Little Miss Salsa simply can't go."

Luckily at about the same time this was happening
I was getting ready to drive back to the Windy City
My truck was already overflowing with numerous pets
But I very gladly found room for this adorable old kitty

And it seems that Little Miss Salsa loved to talk
So she gave me all sorts of back seat driver hell
Every time that I got lost or made a wrong turn
So I think this old kitty cat is pretty darn swell

And a very joyous reunion took place a few days later
Between this re-located family and their beloved cat
I'm sure old Miss Salsa will help ease their anxiety
As they start their new lives I've no doubt about that

But when will our callous government finally learn
That pets are beloved members of so many families?
And when will our extremely slow moving government
Finally end all of this needless pain suffering and misery?

Mangy Dog

"He is your friend, your partner, your defender, your dog.
You are his life, his love, his leader.
He will be yours, faithful and true, to the last beat of his heart.
You owe it to him to be worthy of such devotion."

Author Unknown

I was once again heading south
In very rural southern Mississippi
As I filled my gas tank at the pump
An elderly local woman came up to me

"I see you're with an animal rescue group,
And there's a starving mangy old dog nearby;
He's still faithfully guarding an empty house,
And this loyal old mutt sure makes me want to cry."

So I followed this woman to this nearby dwelling
And the sight of this mangy old dog touched my soul
His humans had abandoned him there in the hurricane
And now he looked like he was very weak and very cold

So I very slowly walked up and approached him there
He was still lying on the shambles of this home's steps
And he truly did appear to be still diligently protecting it
After many many weeks he hadn't relinquished his duties yet

But according to this kindly woman
Her neighbors would definitely not return
So I quietly sat down on the steps with this dog
And offered him a bit of food he seemed to yearn

Eventually I gained sufficient trust from this old guard dog
And he allowed me to lift him up into the safety of my truck
Mangy Dog is recovering very nicely at the camp's Mash Unit
And it's about time this loyal old canine had just a little bit of luck

Violet

***"The fidelity of a dog is a precious gift,
Demanding no less binding moral responsibilities
Than the friendship of a human being.
The bond with a dog,
Is as lasting as the ties of this earth can ever be."***

Konrad Lorenz

She was such a sweet Shepherd
But so horrendously traumatized
She wandered aimlessly in a daze
We could see the trauma in her eyes

When she was brought to the camp
She was listless and would not eat
Soon she just collapsed in a heap
Refusing to even stand on her feet

Hers was not a physical injury
She was truly giving up on her life
She'd been left behind by someone dear
Puncturing her heart and soul like a knife

Many of us soon began to believe
That she'd seen her beloved human die
Now she no longer cared to live herself
And it made so many of us want to cry

But one of the compassionate volunteers
Saw her withering and named her 'Violet'
And he lovingly took her under his wing
Absolutely refusing to give up on her yet

He spent hours with this 'left behind' dog
Attempting to establish a new bond with her
Each and every night comforting her in his tent
Talking soothingly to Violet while stroking her fur

Eventually we began to see a miraculous revival
Violet was eating and at his side would now roam
Many of us in the pet rescue camp were overjoyed
That truly marvelous day - when John took her home

The Old Traveler

"A child on a farm sees a plane fly overhead,
And dreams of faraway places.
A traveler on that plane sees the farmhouse,
And dreams of home."

Carl Burns

I came upon an old grey cat
Who must have journeyed far
His silhouette was very ghostly
He was beaten battered scarred

His head hung low
His coat was torn
His flesh was gaunt
His feet were worn

Yet this traveler traveled on

I offered him a sip of water
He savored it like wine
I offered him a bit of meat
And he ravenously dined

I soon offered him a safe place to rest
And for an instant his gaunt face shined
Then his all consuming yearning sparked
And his extremely haunted eyes declined

Where could he be going
This bitterly cold autumn day
What compelled him forward
I really couldn't say

Was he searching for a loved one
Was he struggling to get home
Was he on a desperate mission
Or was he dying - all alone

I guess I'll never know

As this valiant voyager trudged off
I silently wished him well
I could somehow feel his anguish
I could somehow sense his hell

Yet this traveler traveled on

As I watched this old grey cat vanish
Drenched in both determination and fear
As I watched this old grey cat vanish
I shed yet another tear

- And this traveler traveled on -

One Eyed Jack

***"Dogs, bless them,
Operate on the premise
That human beings are fragile
And require incessant applications
Of affection and reassurance."***

Mary McGrory

He was a gigantic old brown dog
Part Chow and perhaps St. Bernard
And he had the sweetest disposition
Even though Katrina had hit him hard

He had suffered debilitating head trauma
The medical team had to remove one eye
And every time I looked at this injured dog
I nearly broke down and often wanted to cry

He was being housed in a small cage
In the Mash Unit during his recovery
And I found myself visiting every night
This injured mutt had really gotten to me

Since the medical staff was always extremely busy
They asked volunteers to walk these dogs every night
And I always somehow found myself standing by his cage
Before taking One Eyed Jack out for a walk in the moonlight

He and I would pleasantly wander around the camp
He was extremely appreciative and very well behaved
And I think his massive injuries bothered me more than him
He was truly one of the brave souls who faced life so unafraid

And each and every night after our leisurely stroll
When I would carefully place him back inside his pen
He would reward me with very affectionate facial kisses
Gentle One Eyed Jack would kiss me over and over again

I truly miss old One Eyed Jack these days and nights
Since he taught me a most valuable lesson about living
No matter how bad we think that life has been treating us
To others more in need our compassion we should be giving

A Vet and His Pet

***"If you are a host to a man,
Be a host to his dog, too."***

A Russian Proverb

Since I'm a very staunch fan
Of both our veterans and our pets
I really feel compelled to relay
One of the best Katrina reunions yet

William is a very courageous veteran
Who also happens to be a double amputee
When the deep flood waters rose in New Orleans
From his home he had to swim and cling to a tree

With his faithful best friend swimming by his side
William finally managed to reach the roof of his home
But when the rescuers finally arrived to save them both
He was told he would have to leave his dog there all alone

William the distraught vet was airlifted to a veterans' hospital
Hundreds of miles away in Miami which is an extremely big city
William's very loyal friend who somehow managed to survive
Was transported to a pet rescue camp in very rural Mississippi

Two very compassionate volunteers from this pet rescue camp
Drove William's best friend all the way down the coast to Miami
This is one truly marvelous Hurricane Katrina people/pet reunion
Providing both veteran and animal supporters with absolute glee

If you have not already taken the time and the effort to do so
Please sign the petition on the enclosed Humane Society web site
Urging legislators to never again separate humans and their pets
Forcing anyone to leave behind their best friend – is just not right

www.hsus.org

Heavenly Touch

"The dog is the only animal that has seen his god."

Author Unknown

He too had boarded the evacuation bus
Cradled in his master's very loving arms
When suddenly an extremely callous official
Tossed him right off - and straight into harm

As that very crowded bus quickly sped away
I can't imagine the heartbreak in his lonely sighs
Standing out there watching the humans he loved
Suddenly vanishing before his tiny unbelieving eyes

This extremely small extremely terrified apricot poodle
Now had to wander the flooded streets of New Orleans
One minute he had been very safe and warm and cuddled
And the next minute his life had turned so viciously mean

Tiny somehow managed to survive on his own
Until he was rescued by a very compassionate soul
But this once pampered little dog had now lost his gods
And now for him life was still so horribly cruel and cold

But miracles can sometimes happen even for heartbroken poodles
And a distraught young couple had also missed him so very much
The glorious day that they found him we all shed many tears of joy
Since Tiny had again found Paradise – it was in his master's touch

Get Shorty

"A House is not a Home,
Without a Dog."

Anonymous

As I was preparing to leave camp again
An urgent message was suddenly relayed
"Can anyone possibly drive to Alexandria,
To get Shorty to his new home, right away?"

Since I and many others knew Shorty
He was a big gentle Chow mix pup
Before I even knew what I was doing
I had subconsciously yelled out, "Yup!"

So within just a few short minutes
Shorty and several other 'found' pets
Were carefully loaded inside my truck
And I didn't know where Alexandria was yet

As we raced away from the pet rescue camp
I hurriedly studied my huge road atlas map
Learning Alexandria was in western Louisiana
As my animal passengers settled in for a cozy nap

Although the road to Alexandria was quite long
It was filled with back road serenity and beauty
And within about four hours and some minutes
We neared the new home of this Chow pup cutey

And my furry pal Shorty like most of my other passengers
Had not stirred much at all during this very long road journey
But as we drew closer to his family and to his brand new home
Shorty instinctively began displaying a very passionate yearning

Shorty had somehow already known
That his beloved humans were very nearby
And when he spotted the people he truly loved
This sentimental old dog lover nearly started to cry

This family was truly overjoyed
Even Shorty gave me a kiss or two
For both these humans and this canine
Their future days would now be far less blue

This was truly a splendid reunion celebration
For both this re-located family and this Chow
And as I raced away to my next stop in St. Louis
Both of my eyes suddenly began to mist up somehow

Autumn in St. Louis

"Who would believe such pleasure from a wee ball o' fur?"

An Irish Saying

She was an extremely sweet tabby
But she wasn't feeling very well
She was lethargic and refused to eat
This gentle feline had been through hell

We all knew that she truly longed to be home
We all knew that her humans she truly did miss
And we were all overjoyed when the call came in
"Can someone bring our little Autumn to St. Louis?"

So before very long at all
This 'found' cat was in my truck too
And as we raced off towards Missouri
I hoped Autumn would soon be less blue

And I witnessed an amazing transformation
When I carried this kitty through her new door
She very excitedly began yapping and dancing
She had finally found the humans she adored

And within just a very few short minutes
Autumn was eating and purring very contentedly
I now knew that this overjoyed little orange furball
Would adjust to her new life in St. Louis most happily

Halloween Dream

"Dreams are illustrations...
From the book your soul is writing about you."

Marsha Norman

I've been having a very strange dream
About a gigantic feline that I continue to see
I always encounter him on a dark moonless night
And this extremely vivid vision truly captivates me

His fur is very long sleek and coal black
And his eyes are a mesmerizing fire red
I think he's a traveler from a distant realm
And I meet him wandering among the dead

Black cats have usually been associated
With witches spells demons and sorcery
But we humans have demonized them
They are not to blame for this imagery

Is this mysterious creature a friend or foe
And does he truly have a message for me
And even more fascinating for me right now
Is the possibility of meeting him on Halloween

Will I really encounter such a creature
Perhaps at an eerie graveyard that night
The possibility truly does intrigue me
And this vision doesn't fill me with fright

I'm again heading back down to the devastated Gulf Coast
I've decided to help round up more tragically 'left behind' cats
It seems that far too many felines are still in trouble down there
And I wonder if this intriguing feline knows something about that

Halloween Dream, Part II

"Once upon a time, I, Chuang-tzu, dreamt I was a butterfly,
Flittering hither and thither, to all intents and purposes a butterfly.
Suddenly I awoke...
Now I do not know whether I was then a man dreaming I was a butterfly,
Or whether I am now a butterfly, dreaming I am a man."

Chuang-tzu, Chinese Philosopher

Dawn was just now breaking
As I wandered New Orleans
It was Halloween morning
And it truly was an eerie scene

The temperature had dropped overnight
And a very thick pea soup fog had rolled in
I was wandering the old warehouse district
As this new Louisiana day was about to begin

Suddenly I somehow managed to spot him
That intriguing big black cat from my dream
I quickly raced after him down the dark street
He was heading for an old warehouse it seemed

This cat quickly darted behind an old junked car
So I intently peered under this heap with little dread
But this huge mysterious black feline had now vanished
And to my utter amazement I found something else instead

There peering very morosely back up at me
Were two sets of very forlorn puppy eyes
These two young canines were about done in
And finding them was quite a joyous surprise

I scooped them both up in my arms
And raced them back to my warm truck
I hoped that with a little food and water
These two pups would recover with luck

Soon they were both sleeping contentedly
As I drove them back to the pet rescue camp
Had the cat from my dream truly led me to them
Or had I managed to find them strictly by chance

As I pondered over this very intriguing question
I named these two young dogs 'Miss' and 'Sippy'
Since I had found them down by the Mississippi River
On a most captivating Halloween morning quite nippy

And these two adorable brown and white Katrina puppies
Soon became the joyous focus of my pet rescue Halloween
One of the volunteers soon dressed them up in party costumes
And now - they had mysteriously become two black cats it seems

Eddie

***"I will survive,
Oh as long as I know how to love I know I'll stay alive;
I've got all my life to live,
I've got all my love to give, and I'll survive,
I will survive."***

I Will Survive,
Gloria Gaynor

He arrived at our rescue camp one night
Barely alive and in a truly horrifying state
He had been on the mean streets for many weeks
He was emaciated de-hydrated and terribly afraid

I opened his crate and I was truly saddened
Both of his eyes were grotesquely swollen shut
Thick dried gobs of white saliva hung from his jowls
This starving 'left behind' canine was about to give up

I gently coaxed him from his constraining carrier
And he hobbled forward and collapsed into my arms
I sat in the dirt with this barely alive creature for hours
Gently trying to convince him that he was now out of harm

When morning finally arrived I left him there
Sleeping very fitfully in his 'safe haven' pen
Sadly wondering if this dog had the will to survive
Sadly wondering if this orphan would ever rise again

Several hours later as I stood near his pen talking to someone
Someone else yelled out that he was now intently listening to me
Suddenly he rose on his wobbly legs and meekly wagged his tail
So they all applauded and immediately named this dog 'Eddie'

They say that sometimes animals truly do choose their humans
And I'm definitely a person who has always believed this is true
So of course the re-vitalized dog 'Eddie' came home in my truck
I'm still trying to convince my wife there was little else I could do

And in the course of the several weeks he's been living with us
'Eddie' truly has become a very different and mischievous pup
He delights in wrestling with Turbo Dog and terrorizing our cats
And chewing everything non edible then humorously barfing it up

I eventually started calling him 'Turbo Junior'
Since his antics remind me so much of our mutt
Then I eventually began calling him 'Goofball'
But his forever permanent name hasn't yet stuck

And of course my name around here is once again 'Mud'
For bringing a third extremely uncivilized canine into our home
I'm now living in the doghouse with Eddie Turbo and tiny Blanca
Hoping for a reprieve soon so all four of us can wrestle and roam

Even worse Buddy the Cat just like my lovely wife
Is extremely upset and truly fed up with me right now
But I really want to get back in both of their good graces
And I know that I will – some day – some way – somehow

Where's Tater?

"Bad boys, bad boys,
Whatcha gonna do, whatcha gonna do,
When they come for you?"

Bad Boys Theme Song

An e-mail had arrived at the pet rescue camp
From a small demolition crew down in Gulfport
They had been feeding a starving abandoned dog
And they reported that he was really a friendly sort

They had been tossing this young starving dog French fries
He was a very gentle Lab pup they had soon named 'Tater'
And what a comical picture they had taken of him racing by
So I jumped in my truck and shouted out, "See you all later!"

As I drove the 100 plus miles down to Gulfport
I kept wondering if I could truly capture this pup
Very sadly this demolition crew was now moving on
And no one would remain there to gives this dog sup

When I finally arrived at the devastated trailer park
I didn't see any abandoned canines hanging around
And now I very sadly stared at the picture in front of me
Wondering if this 'left behind' dog would ever be found

But as I slowly drove past a huge pile of trash
A black Labrador puppy suddenly dashed out
I quickly opened my truck door and whistled
Knowing this had to be 'Tater' without a doubt

As I stood there by that trash pile whistling loudly
Tater came bounding up and leaped into my truck
This was really one friendly little starving canine
With a determined survival instinct not to give up

In the next four days of roaming the southland
Tater and I quickly became the best of friends
He and I slept in the truck every night together
He rode shotgun with me diligently without end

But I had also fervently swore and vowed to my lovely wife
That I wouldn't be bringing home any more animals this time
Yet the cunning Tater had somehow stowed away in my truck
And now we have both been accused of a most diabolical crime

I also fear that I may now be in my wife's permanent 'dog house'
But I've noticed that she's quickly falling for this puppy's charm
And I don't know if anyone can possibly resist a little tater or two
Especially one so adorably delightful and so joyously out of harm

Bad boys, bad boys,
Whatcha gonna do, whatcha gonna do,
When you married one, too?

Rain Puddles

"When the well is dry, we learn the worth of water."

Benjamin Franklin

I went sauntering in the woods yesterday
With four very eager inquisitive canines
It was a spectacularly peaceful autumn day
With a magnificent briskness in the air divine

The brilliant yellow sun was gloriously shining
Colorful leaves danced throughout the forest floor
The many woodland birds were merrily serenading us
An old nature loving man like me couldn't ask for more

It was also another truly wondrous learning experience for me
As I joyfully watched four happy playful dogs rushing all about
There was a distinct difference between my two loyal old mutts
And the actions of these two new Katrina pups without a doubt

It had rained quite heavily just the prior evening
And there were huge wet rain puddles everywhere
My two old dogs hardly gave them a second glance
But at each and every puddle these Katrina dogs stared

First they would both immediately stop at each and every puddle
Then they would both sniff and savor the water's heavenly smell
Finally they would both eagerly lap up as much as they could drink
Obviously now remembering their recent fresh water scarcity hell

And before long all five of us began frolicking and splashing
In these heaven sent rain puddles as we joyously ran and roamed
And I knew I'd never take nature's gift of H2O for granted again
As I treated us all to more heavenly water when we returned home

A Flower Blooms in Winter

"I love cats because I love my home,
And after a while they become its visible soul."

Jean Cocteau

When I first brought our little Flower home
She remained aloof and distant for quite awhile
She had sadly lost her siblings in the hurricane
And she'd traveled more than a thousand miles

Her eyes still seemed quite distant
She was still quite timid and afraid
She had never known love or friendship
So in these waters she had hesitated to wade

But within a relatively short period of time
Our dear old tabby Buddy befriended her
And these days I often spot Flower with him
Her tiny yap sounding much more like a purr

She also now naps in our bedroom with Tuffy
Who had also once been an orphan and a stray
Little Tuffy truly seems to enjoy her company
And the two of them have now begun to play

She's also become very inquisitive about me
As she now follows me all around the house
And her stalking skills are really improving
As she tiptoes after me as craftily as a mouse

But the most wondrous thing of all has just occurred
She's begun silently crawling up on our bed each night
And she has just now discovered my wife's loving touch
As she snuggles ever closer with contentment and delight

This once extremely sad and lonely Katrina victim
Is thankfully now beginning to blossom and to bloom
And now my spouse is very glad that I brought her home
Since she believes that winter flowers truly brighten any room

Help!

***"Help, I need somebody,
Help, not just anybody,
Help, you know I need someone, help."***

Help!
The Beatles

Thousands of dogs and cats
Have been tragically left behind
And now they truly need more help
From anyone who is the least bit kind

Sadly there have not been very many reunions
Between 'left behind pets' and their human beings
So the vast majority of these homeless dogs and cats
Are now being sent all across this vast country it seems

Tragically some of their owners died in the storm
And many have now re-located and moved away
And many of them simply are no longer allowed
To keep pets in the new dwellings where they stay

So we are now sending thousands of 'left behind' hurricane pets
To animal shelters and humane societies all across this vast land
And if you can find it in your heart to help at least one of them
Your gesture of kindness and compassion would be truly grand

Please contact your local shelters and humane societies
To determine if any hurricane pets have arrived these days
Then perhaps you will be able to foster one or two of them
Or at least send some sort of monetary donation their way

Caring for these animals is very expensive
And most animal shelters rely on donations
Supporting your local animal shelters now
Would truly help them in this dire situation

"Help me if you can, I'm feeling down,
And I do appreciate you being round.
Help me get my feet back on the ground,
Won't you please, please, help me."

Paradise Lost

"The greatness of a nation,
And its moral progress,
Can be judged,
By the way its animals are treated."

Gandhi

Dogs first befriended man
Many thousands of years ago
And cats since the days of ancient Egypt
Have managed to purr their way into our souls

Yet somewhere along mankind's long line of history
We somehow lost our respect for these noble creatures
The callous way that we very often treat them these days
Is surely not one of modern man's most redeeming features

Months after Hurricane Katrina wreaked her destruction
There are still many starving dogs and cats on the coast
And many of them have now turned untrusting and wild
Having been forsaken by beings they had loved the most

Once very faithful dogs have now formed wild packs
After being abandoned by their once trusted human friends
And once very content domesticated cats have now gone feral
On their ancient survival instincts they've been forced to depend

And these once very docile and trusting 'left behind' pets
Will most likely never be able to trust we human beings again
What we all permitted to happen to them in Hurricane Katrina
Is surely not a very proud legacy to future generations we send

Far too many of these once cared for and domesticated animals
Now live out their days in the desperate shadows where they die
Both from starvation and by being killed by uncaring civilization
And these are the images that now haunt every pet rescuer's eyes

We rescuers pray that our government has now grown a lot wiser
We pray owners will never again be forced to leave them behind
We pray that we've all learned a lesson from Hurricane Katrina
For the torment in their 'left behind' eyes lives on in our minds

A Rescuer's Prayer

Hear our humble prayer, O God,
For our friends the animals,
especially for animals who are suffering;
for any that are hunted or lost
or deserted or frightened or hungry;
and for all that must be put to sleep.

We entreat for them all
Thy mercy and pity,
and for those who deal with them
we ask a heart of compassion,
and gentle hands, and kindly words.

Make us be true friends to animals,
and so to share,
the blessings of the world.

Dr. Albert Schweitzer

Acknowledgements and Thanks

Following Hurricane Katrina, thousands of extremely compassionate caring people from all around the world, and from all walks of life, literally poured into the devastated areas along the Gulf Coast.

Many of them brought their own rescue equipment and supplies and vehicles - and without a doubt their inherent compulsion and undying passion to help. And they often surrendered their vacation time, their own finances, and their personal comfort to rescue both people and animals, and to find suitable shelter for thousands of each in both Louisiana and Mississippi, and soon, far beyond.

I met dozens of extremely compassionate caring individuals on my journeys to the hurricane ravaged Gulf Coast – both human rescuers and animal rescuers. And I am truly blessed to have met each of them because they have renewed my faith in mankind.

So many of these individuals were extraordinarily tireless in their valiant efforts to help both our human and our nonhuman neighbors in this truly horrific catastrophe.

Besides the untold human grief and suffering resulting from Hurricane Katrina, this was the largest animal rescue effort ever launched in the United States, and the numbers are staggering.

The American Veterinary Medical Association estimates that 40-50,000 pets lived in New Orleans alone prior to Hurricane Katrina.

Tens of thousands of these pets tragically died in the storm, but over 10,000 of these 'left behind' animals were compassionately rescued in Louisiana and Mississippi; and they were rescued by individuals working on their own, and by individuals affiliated with organized animal rescue groups and humane societies either as staff members or as volunteers.

Numerous pet rescue camps and temporary animal shelters were quickly established throughout the Gulf Coast shortly after Hurricane Katrina wreaked her havoc by animal welfare organizations such as the *Humane Society of the United States, Noah's Wish, the Kinship Circle, Alley Cat Allies*, the *Best Friends Animal Society*, and many others.

I met many individuals from many of these groups, and I deeply admire them all. I also met many individuals who worked on their own – because they felt compelled to, with no group or financial support whatsoever – and I truly admire their extremely valiant and compassionate actions.

When I wasn't out rescuing animals, I spent much of my time at the *Best Friends Pet Rescue Camp* located on the *St. Francis Animal Sanctuary* grounds in Tylertown, Mississippi; and in my opinion, this was one of the best run pet rescue operations on the Gulf Coast.

Many of the stories in this book revolve around this pet rescue camp, and I am truly honored to have met so many of the wonderful staff members and volunteers working there.

I've been affiliated with *Best Friends* for several years now, participating in their *National Pet Network*, often transporting adopted animals to new homes for them. And, hopefully, my volunteer work with *Best Friends* will continue.

I also became very good friends with several individuals working in Tylertown, and I hope to continue my friendship with them as well. They know who they are, so I won't mention any names, for fear I might leave a name or two out.

But thank you all from the bottom of my heart – it was my greatest pleasure meeting each of you, working with each of you, and getting to know so many other people who share such a deep passion and concern for our extremely loyal, and very often helpless, nonhuman neighbors.

I would also like to extend my sincere appreciation to anyone involved at all, in any way, in the massive international Hurricane Katrina pet rescue effort - from the young grade school children who eagerly collected donations for these animals; to friends and neighbors who generously collected pet supplies or sent cash donations to rescue groups; to the veterinarians and humane societies who donated their time and supplies; to the countless valiant individuals who rushed to the Gulf Coast on their own; to these established pet rescue organizations; and most of all, to my very understanding and loving wife.

I had promised her that I wouldn't bring back any 'left behind' Katrina pets since I somehow manage to bring home enough orphans and strays in our own area.

And I quickly broke my solemn promise to her, bringing home three very needy hurricane orphans who had quickly managed to wag and purr their way into my heart and soul.

Her only consolation is knowing that hundreds of other animal loving people also broke their promises to their extremely understanding mates, and brought many of these adorable animals home as well.

But there are still thousands of these 'left behind' Katrina pets now being cared for at animal shelters and humane societies all across the U.S. To date, only about one tenth of them have been successfully reunited with their pre-Katrina human friends.

Some of their owners tragically died in the storm, and countless numbers of their former owners have now re-located to distant areas and states or to dwellings which will not allow them to keep pets.

And this is truly not the fault of any of these precious animals, whose lives were so horribly disrupted, too.

Perhaps you might find it in your heart and soul to let one of these very deserving pets purr or wag their way into your life. There might be one waiting just for you, at an animal shelter or humane society near your home.

These tragically 'left behind' nonhuman neighbors of ours would be forever in your debt; as would I and every other individual who rushed to the Gulf Coast and soon peered into their extremely forlorn, truly devastated, and completely heartbroken, Katrina eyes.

About the Author

Ed Kostro is an animal and nature lover, shelter volunteer, feral feline trapper, and now, a Hurricane Katrina pet rescuer. He's also a published animal and nature writer whose credits include *Chicken Soup for the Dog Lover's Soul, Cats Do It Better than People, Catholic Digest, Pet Life, Pets: part of the family*, and numerous other publications.

He has now written five books, including a Western; a time travel/adventure novel set in the Canadian wilderness; a middle reader adventure story for young boys set in modern day Arizona; and his nonfiction life's memoir entitled *Curious Creatures-Wondrous Waifs, My Life with Animals*. This book was awarded a *Certificate of Excellence* in the *2004 International Cat Writers' Association Communication Contest.*

All of Ed's books, and many of his poems, stories, and articles can be found on his writing website:

www.authorsden.com/edkostro

Ed currently resides in Illinois with his wife Rebecca, and several rescued dogs and cats, including three 'left behind' hurricane pets he recently brought home from the Gulf Coast.

CPSIA information can be obtained
at www.ICGtesting.com
Printed in the USA
LVHW04s1549280918
591696LV00001B/7/P

9 781591 138679